Success Is Never Ending

Given to _____

On this _____ day of _____

By _____

With this special message . . .

_____

_____

_____

Success Is Never Ending

Inspiration from
Robert H. Schuller

THOMAS NELSON
PUBLISHERS

Published in Nashville, Tennessee by
Thomas Nelson Publishers.

**Library of Congress
Cataloging-in-Publication Data**

Schuller, Robert Harold.
    Success Is Never Ending / Robert H.
Schuller.
        p.   cm. — (Itty Bitty book)
    ISBN 0-8407-6307-7 (TR)
    ISBN 0-7852-8262-9 (MM)
    1. Success—Religious
aspects—Quotations, maxims, etc.
I. Title   II. Series.
BV4598.3.S387   1993
242—dc20   93-18293
                                    CIP

Printed in Hong Kong
1 2 3 4 5 6 7 — 98 97 96 95 94 93

Success Is Never Ending

Success is a
journey . . .
not a destination.

A Year from Now You May Wish You Had Started Today.

———

Faith, focus and followthrough are the 3 key words to success!

EVERY BEGINNER IS A WINNER.

Progress is . . .
turning
impossibilities into
possibilities!

COMPROMISE
IS KINGLY.

Success is not escaping problems but facing them creatively.

FAILURE DOESN'T MEAN YOU SHOULD GIVE UP . . . IT DOES MEAN YOU NEED TO TRY HARDER.

Never surrender leadership to problems.

THERE IS NO SUCCESS WITHOUT SACRIFICE.

Triumph is made up
of two words: try . . .
and . . . umph.

EVERY OBSTACLE IS A POTENTIAL OPPORTUNITY.

Even failure can become an important ingredient to success.

PLAN YOUR DAY AND WORK YOUR PLAN.

You will never be licked if you know what you lack.

FAILURE JUST MEANS THAT YOU HAVE NOT YET SUCCEEDED.

Growth is always marked by difficulties.

I'D RATHER CHANGE MY MIND AND SUCCEED THAN HAVE MY OWN WAY AND FAIL.

Don't fix
the blame . . .
fix the problem.

THE REAL CRIME IS NOT FAILURE BUT LOW AIM.

Put down your failure. Start again! It can be fun, it can be done!

SUCCESS WITHOUT CONFLICT IS UNREALISTIC.

Any person can be successful on smooth seas—but—it is the victor over the storm who gains true honor.

FAILURES ARE ONLY PROBLEMS WAITING TO BE SOLVED!

Success is noblest
when it leaves you
with self-respect.

NEVER STOP
AT THE TOP!

Patience and persistence are the crowning qualities of self-confident champions.

GREAT SUCCESS ALWAYS CALLS FOR GREAT SACRIFICE.

Success doesn't come through the way you think it comes, it comes through the way you think.

NEVER SETTLE FOR LESS THAN SUCCESS.

Success is doing
something good . . .
when you can . . .
where you can . . .
while you can.

NEVER LET A PROBLEM BECOME AN EXCUSE.

Don't throw a curtain across tomorrow . . . the star of its performance just may <u>be you</u>!

Nothing Great Ever Happens on the O.K. Level.

Impossible situations
can become
challenges that
beckon great
possibilities.

REAL FAILURE IS FAILING TO MAKE THE MOST OF THE GIFTS GOD HAS GIVEN YOU.

There is no gain without pain.

TODAY'S ACCOMPLISHMENTS WERE YESTERDAY'S IMPOSSIBILITIES.

Press on . . .
obstacles are
seldom the same
size tomorrow as
they are today.

It's better to attempt to do something great and fail, than attempt to do nothing and succeed.

IT TAKES GUTS TO LEAVE THE RUTS!

Reach Out . . .
Just a Little
Beyond Your
Presumed Abilities.

With each new
peak scaled, channel
your imagination
toward envisioning
new fields to conquer.

AIM AT NOTHING AND YOU *WILL* SUCCEED.

———

Talent is spelled W-O-R-K.

SUCCESS IS NEVER ENDING—AND—FAILURE NEVER FINAL.

Manage your misses by learning from every failure.

GREAT
THINGS
HAPPEN WHEN
GOD AND YOU
CONFRONT A
MOUNTAIN.

Success is not necessarily reaching your goal— BUT—reaching the maximum possibilities in light of the opportunities that come your way.

If you fail to plan,

you are planning

to fail!

To succeed, you have to grab hold of God's dreams.

You will not quit.
You will keep up
your brave
performance
because the very
power of the eternal
God surges deep
within your being.

Success can be defined as bearing fruit (being productive) and fulfilling God's plan for our lives.

THE BIGGEST
PROBLEM YOU FACE
IS FINDING
YOURSELF
SURROUNDED
WITH MORE
OPPORTUNITIES

THAN YOU CAN
HANDLE.
GIVE YOUR
BEST TIME TO
YOUR
MOST IMPORTANT
PROJECTS.

———

SUCCESS IS ACHIEVING THE MAXIMUM OF YOUR POTENTIAL IN THE SITUATION THAT YOU ARE IN.

At the Bottom Line of Business, There Are No Numbers, Only People.

To keep your values on target, remember to live so that when you "arrive," you'll have pride behind you,

and hope ahead of
you. Then success
is truly the path
to heaven.

Make certain that your decisions are based upon problems that beg for solutions and not upon your own ego needs.

THE SECRET OF SUCCESS IS TO FIND A NEED AND FILL IT.

Success keeps moving on and failures are only temporary setbacks.

Always Remember: "Failures" Are Only Problems Waiting to Be Solved!

Failure is never final to the person who has a healthy self-regard. Success is never ending to the person

who keeps believing,
"I've got a lot to offer
and I've still got a lot
to give. Next time I'll
make it!"

———

YOUR NUMBER ONE JOB IS TO MAKE CERTAIN THAT YOU ARE A POSSIBILITY THINKER!

———

Success Might Be Possible If You Don't Try to Achieve It All by Yourself.

Say good-bye
to failure and say
hello to success.
Reprogram yourself
to think positively
and to look for
the possibilities.

You Deserve to Be a Success. You Do! You Deserve the Best!

———

Use the magic words, "It might be possible! I don't know how, or when, but it might be possible!"

PLAN TO KEEP WINNING! THE "NEXT TIME" ALWAYS MOTIVATES YOU TO KEEP TRYING.

SUCCESS IS
NEVER ENDING
BECAUSE
SUCCESS IS
LIKE THE
PROCESS OF
SEED
PLANTING. . .

EVERY
CREATIVE,
REDEMPTIVE
CONTRIBUTION,
LIKE A SEED
PLANTED,
WILL BEAR
FRUIT.

———

Remember: the eagle stirs up the nest in order that the young might learn to fly! Your trouble may be your greatest opportunity.

Believe It and You Will Achieve It!

IT IS NEVER TOO LATE TO LEARN AND TO GROW. THERE ARE EXCITING NEW DISCOVERIES BEING MADE

EVERY DAY
THAT CAN
HELP US IN
OUR QUEST TO
BE ALL THAT
WE ARE MEANT
TO BE.

———

Give yourself a pat on the back. It's true you made mistakes. But there were things you did right! You deserve a pat on the back.

I deserve the best! I deserve to succeed, I deserve to have happy, fulfilling relationships.

A PLAN IS
ALL-IMPORTANT
AND IT CANNOT
BE JUST ANY
PLAN; IT
NEEDS TO BE
A POSITIVE
PLAN! I'VE

SAID IT ONCE;
I'LL SAY IT
AGAIN — WHEN
YOU FAIL TO
PLAN YOU
PLAN TO FAIL!

When you realize that the worst that can happen is that you may have to face a disappointment,

then you will be
transformed from a
doubter to a
believer, from a
negative thinker to a
positive thinker.

Family is the key to success. Family promotes a safe place. It gives the freedom to dream dreams and set goals.

Love sanctifies

success.

———

Everyone Faces
Disappointments
At One Time or
Another—But The
Winners Are The
Ones Who Refuse

TO LET
DISAPPOINTMENTS
BECOME
DISCOURAGEMENTS.

Success, finally, is not what you have . . . it is not what you do . . . it is who you are—children of the living God!